THE TIME IT TAKES TO DROWN

THE TIME IT

TAKES TO DROWN

RACHEL E. KRUMENACKER

WALNUT STREET
—PUBLISHING—

ISBN 979-8-9893320-4-5

Walnut Street Publishing
1645 S Holtzclaw Ave
Chattanooga, TN 37404

We look at the world once, in childhood. The rest is memory.

—Louise Gluck, "Nostos"

TABLE OF CONTENTS

CATALOG OF THINGS LOST

From the next room I hear my father's voice...
a sound so sad I think he must be
reliving a catalog of things lost...
Natasha Trethewey, *"Fouled"*

Before we had to unlearn hugs, before

hands draped across our bodies sent us

shuddering, flinching from touch,

we hushed our voices to say *fuck*

like we whispered bedtime prayers.

Our legs restless unfelt unclean. Before,

we wore lace at our throats and ankles,

bobby socks stained white with Jesus' blood,

preachers filled the extremes of FM radio,

warning of violence from someone who

lived in our hearts. Our girlhood shirtless

unshaven un-skinbroken. Before the Bible Belt

meant leather limp in the closets where we hid,

we feared hell more than we loved god.

Our fathers not in heaven, but on earth,

issuing their commandments against us, his hard-
hearted

Pharaohs. Our bodies created to be temples

yet no worshippers let in.

FOURTH OF JULY

You smell of fireworks' sulfur, flushed with
magnolia spirit,

heavy-lidded and heart-hungover from the
unbearable

intimacy of porches. You offer your shoulder for
my head

as the street lamps slur, awed I would trust you

with my worst possession. Crossettes silhouette

an incline aflame. You dig your fingers into

balsa-wood bones soaked in gin,

crack wide my ribs like oyster lips.

You loose the contents of your quiver

into kidneys, your gaze a clinical, exacting fire

that turns my goosebumps to stain-glass windows.
You spear me cervix to cortex.

We weep together, but you first.

HOMETOWN HEADLINE

"Amish Woman Swept Away in Flash Flood"

reaches national news. Everyone assumes Gaea

spares her righteous, rightful caretakers

from these fates, but Earth adores adopting
familiars,

returning unto her those she claimed her own.

____ deserved a better obituary I cannot write.

Her family asks no public mourning,

no photos of the dead posted online,

Personal blogs preserving her likeness.

No digital record of her life remains but this.

Growing up rural means nothing if you never

leave mom's basement. Ashes to ashes,

dust to mud; her body reunites with crickbed,

but not where anyone can find it. Her mother

runs a bath while her sons scour churning banks,

dressed in Sunday's best fishing waders, hunting
vests.

Lavender tubwater laps against the shoals

of her ribcage; tinted water transforming bloated
bellies

Into murky tide pools. Recalls the day they first
met—

liquor amnii pouring down shared thighs, muscles

seized in expectation, exaltation, contraction—!

With measured breaths, she finds comfort
remembering,

how even in the womb, her daughter swam.

FEVER, 2020

I miss hairy legs in sundrunk air, forget

the purpose of doing, glimpse

purpling mountains hazy with dusk

and distance. I miss remembering

the point of being sober, the slow crawl

from a wound I stitched inside myself.

Wine warms the back of my neck the way

whispers never could. Slowly I succumb

to lidded eyes, sipping overflowing cups

easily as water. Gulping, guzzling boozy marrow

streaming from the pierced slit in my side.

P{S}ALM READING

Farmhands begat coal miners begat steel workers

begat me; calloused lilywhite, wringing hands,

upturnt towards sunlight, crying out their blood

will not to suffer forever; their sweatlabour not
spent

in vain. Homemakers' bleachbone, aching fingers

trace vellum-etched letters after sunset, the
insomniac

candle illuminating their grandchild's manuscripts.

Agony sounds out meanings ascribed to arbitrary

Symbols, misunderstandings pressed into lines

with every postmodern translation. My ancestors

study, against all skill and energy, after heaving
boulders

twelve-hour days, six on, one off; now hunched

o'er kitchen tables in agony and strength. Desperate
to regain what they sacrificed to till the land,
make life better for yet unborn descendants.
The unknown that comes after they leave.

ON MOVING HOUSE (AGAIN)

They teach you of loss, but not how to leave

behind walls that housed your most-loathed,

unlovely parts for years. Uncomfortable daily
ennui

prompted by mom's third text of the day:

your childhood disassembled; bedroom

packed safely into basement boxes

should you ever need to visit home again.

Blessed be those that receive a second chance

at family. The soft, sucking stick

of bare feet against dirty linoleum

haunts dreams where I can't run

fast enough, safely lock my door.

I never meant someone else's small town
to be my final resting place. No house
this side of waking able to confine us two
in harmony within its walls any longer.

THE TIME IT TAKES TO DROWN

A strong drink no longer makes a dent

in my sobriety. Me, liquor and god

can't all fit in the same clay jar; an ouroboros

of ego, poison roiling in my stomach's pit.

You learn a helplessness eagerly awaiting

your own apocalypse. Why love the world now,

when one day eternal oblivion will perfect it?

Not so much losing memories as not making any
more.

Supplication: the act of begging mercy at your
aggressor's knees.

Mine bruise from praying to glass-eyed, doll-dead
reflections.

Horse -bridled and -blinded, my own hand's mercy

leads me from distillery waters begging me to drink.

YOUNG LOVE

My ring-necked pheasant,

     your bones—how aware of mine!—

formed the caryatid

     where I built my shrine.

ON GRIEF

Telling more people doesn't dilute pain nor truth,

only mystifies it. How *do* I feel. How do you want
me to feel,

and why are you never satisfied with my answer?

The busyness of a peaceful death adjusts to the
living's schedule.

The ongoing finality of living. What I'd give for
one restful day

of oblivion. We leave instructions, but tire of
holding space

for those who have left. Maybe after I've gone
you'll commit

to loving me like I asked.

ORPHEUS AND EURYDICE

Young and politely aimless, yet ascetic in the
saintly way—

We white-knuckled our hands into knots, lilting
gay liturgies on

the sweet, suckling air of pondscum summers,
floating downriver

on inner tubes blown full of the only breaths we
shared in daylight.

At dusk, after fireflies worm their way between our
hooked jaws,

our secret selves drown in the drought-receding
shallows

as you pull your hand from mine. Eyes downcast to
sidewalk cracks,

you hustle, wet flipflops slapping a block ahead so
no one could tell

you were with me, knew I'd follow you to earth's
end regardless,

Never able to understand the world from your point
of view.

Doomed eternally to peer parallel, across tandem
hemispheres,

from opposite sides of the same tarnished coin.

RIP VAN GOGH, YOU WOULD'VE LOVED VAPE PENS

Eating yellow paint proved to be urban legend,

old Facebook wives' tales; though to be sure,

the man needed prescriptions. Science.

What I think life means: diligence, apologizing.

When taught how to engage with the world,

I became weeping, guarded; unaware who I am

and always was, deserved love.

I do not care whether you take this as confessional or

comic relief; my friends text wherever they arrive safely.

During panic attacks, I repeat their names

until sobbing recedes to natural breath,

We pet our cats, mutually, unspeaking,
Engrossed in our respective, interwoven lives.
Hoping the silence never ends.

COLLEGE POETRY CLUB, EN MEMORIUM

I found the drafts we wrote cuddled on tattered
couches,
our self-worth placed in odd company and
curb-found treasures, rollback deals.
Sardonic, hot takes that didn't age well,

Bukowski lovers as we all were back then—
Unflattering, purple prose vignettes of those
Unkindly depicted as Unlike us:
Walmart shoppers of ill repute, poor
in spirit, the morally absent. Regular people.

Mediocrity a fate we hoped to avoid,
but not knowing what could unravel our futures
Based on individual genetic codes. No one knew
how badly the others wanted to die yet.

On our first and last date, flustered by talk,

you stopped the car dead at a green light.

I pointed, you laughed, we drove on.

Sometimes I see you cross the road in town;

my fondest, holiest of ghosts I rejoice to see.

AUTOCOMPLETE (TEXTS UNSENT)

I'm fine. I'm fine. Please stop calling me. Give my
love to grandma. Remember when I begged for
your attention? Sometimes I confuse your car's
squeaking brakes for sparrow calls. There's a nest
outside my window now, where mockingbirds spar
jays for dominion over this small corner of our
household, drawing blood over who it's meant to
serve. This reminds me of you. Birds remind me of
me. I heard; I didn't know them well. I'm sorry.

GAY AGENDA

Paradox: bourbonfat business owners

wish I didn't exist, yet profit off my pride
regardless;

Abomination too cool a name for the girl

sucking down ramen in a rented room,

drinking away what brain cells god knit for her,

not fearing any celestial wrath,

                     but mother's omnipresent one.

The matron admits, knees pressed to her
youngest's,

I don't think the gays are bad, yet in the same
breath,

How can you support them? Were they weaker
women,

They could confess—

                     godforsaken bitch

fresh on the lips of roommates cursing me

in diaries I read behind their backs. As my mother

read mine. The only way we knew to ask

if other's emotions got the better of them, too.

I know you are, but what am I?

spat at sleeping forms in unwashed sheets,

depression still a private, all-encompassing fear;

the devil I knew all along, ever-threatening

to drag me screaming, against best intentions,

to a hell I wanted to deserve.

My father texts daily to ask who I'm with,

what I'm doing. I've never lied successfully.

I can't respond: taking meds, then a shower. '

Trying not to write my story's end tonight.

WE YELLED AT WOLVES

risking to howl and be heard

knowing they chased our throats either way

AUTOCOMPLETE

(written with the iOS QuickType feature)

and I don't know what I want to do with my life but I don't want to do

anything with my life but I don't want to do anything

and I was told that I was a good person, and I thought it was a good idea

to be a good person, and I was a good person

five years later he was a good friend of course he was

I can see the way I want you back

to the person you are, the person

you are and you are the best person

I'm not sure if I can get it to work

but he is my favorite person

and now all I want is to be a good person

25

and I will be happy to be with you, and

I don't have to be good to be with you,

but I don't want to be good

he's just got a little more than a lot to do with my
life

lol I don't know what I want to be
but I'm still here for you

CHATTANOOGA NATIONAL CEMETERY

And I wrote how I envisioned the old Romantics
did,
in my single family home, late-due on rent again.
Desk facing autumn window at dusk,
last season cider mimicking mama's foot

against some floor bassinet. The tart rock of sleep,
cradling another sweaty "last" whiskey in leaded
hands.
Old-fashioned glass falling when my wrist slips,
denting cured, post-war floorboards.

Rows of polished military graves wink between
dining-car embouchures. Uniform, fabric-
embellished teeth
beckoning from veteran ancestors who laid down
lives

for promises I could never keep.

Exaggerated, whip-sharp shadows crack downhill
the brown lawns; lightning striking earth from
naked, sleeping boughs. Not even the best
groundskeeper keeps round-the-clock watch
against the drought of the American South,

longing to see it be made great again.
Our fathers, and their fathers before them
planted orchards in calculated, metric
expectation, when rainfall could still be

predicted. When their poet-sons would finally
hitch rides home, tired of time spent away.
My own former warrior jokes, whenever we
pass his fellow fallen, "Rachel, how many

people you think live down in that graveyard?"
No matter the size, publicity of park or plot, I
dutifully respond, grand-daughterhood
fulfilled, "None, Papa. They're all dead."

AUTOBIOGRAPHY (PHARMAKON)

I.
   REMEDY

Children crowd around an old tube tv,

(the cancer-causing kind,

last Gen's leadpaint chewtoys,

asbestos leaking open-mouthed

from unfurnished basement

ceilings). The program's host,

a self-professed born-again

pre-schooler, recites her script:

humanity's last, only defense

before the devil takes over:

sign over your heart's lease

unto Jesus. I, a full year senior,

grow jealous someone younger

learned life's elusive meaning.

Thirty voices chant sinners' prayers.
Most barely understand addition,
how shoes work. Herded into
pens of plastic chairs, divided
M&M's, cheese crackers around squat,
laminate formica tables.
Our portion of the two fish,
five loaves. I search for my parents
amongst the throng pressed bodily
against glass nursery doors,
the mob rescuing their tiresome,
unsettling darlings from
Kid's Sermon shepherds.

Left alone that night

in a bed too big for me,

I ponder hell for the first time.

If I should die before I wake.

II. POISON

Midwinter sleepaway camp, where exhausted
white parents

pay nine hundred Bucks to ship highschoolers

to twelve cabins nestled against ski slopes, named

after Israel's colonizing sons, or Judas' postmortem
friends.

Our lives entrusted to whoever volunteered

to drive the rented bus. At altar call,

one of the hot, older boys known for teasing girls

who cut short their hair,

    "what can I grab onto, then?,"

moved to tears, tracked the metal aisle

of folding chairs, Moses parting Red Seas,

And we all followed, hoping he would lead

our youth group to deliverance

from our perceived oppressors.

Those who victimized us.

A weight lifts off my sore shoulders, ascending

heavenward, hoping vulnerability would

no longer cost my soul.

III. SCAPEGOAT

Growing up gay in the church: years of our brains marinating

In theology like Philadelphia rum-soaked hams. Grandma's

Easter dinner calls for a pound of potatoes per person;

arbitrary etiquette, passed around like common sense.

"Writing what I know" narrows its focus to my mirror.

Maybe my biggest sin was loneliness so vast

not even an omnipotent god had enough love to give.

The irony of fire and brimstone raining, reigning

above pulpits. Televangelists bellow tongue-holstered

sermons with no bearing on reality, foundationless as

temples they built upon sand. Coastlines rise.

The wine and loneliness changed our communion,

but only how rivers resculpt canyons: an evolutionary myth,

that Creation possesses ability to change. A draft re-edited.

That's what all gods and artists want, right,

to create with impunity? Michaelangelo painstakingly frees

the voiceless, godsent hunk from marbled nudity,

with the same diligence it takes to tread water,

waiting for my mother to call Sunday afternoons.

The only forgiveness I seek comes from her.

When I speak to those outside my religion,

I hear I narrowly escaped a cult.

Help me understand where we went wrong.

ORACLE

You say the ocean's rising/like I give a shit/You say the whole world's ending

/honey, it already did

Bo Burnham, "All Eyes on Me"

And I became Apollo's Cassandra: oracle

of doubt, self-appointed to read between

biblical lines. Loudest missionary of absolute,

unquestionable truth. A lot of bottled rage

needed to break over my head before

I stopped believing I could walk on water.

I rattle my prison bars in Delphi's sinking temple;

Those in power refuse to see the signs of the gods.

My life under no microscope holds water, yet

I feel scraped across specimen glass; buttered bread

38

we all ration 'til payday. The bleeding call for
alms,

beg Samaritans' salvation while tax collectors

support the latest war from megachurches' offering
plates.

We didn't expect to die—instead, promised fiery,

heavenward chariots as a martyr's reward for a
pure life

unlived. I remain delusional: who would name me
prophet

of the damned, thousands of black sheep happily
abandoned

for a predestined flock.If I censor my words so
you'll love me,

do we even know each other? I already spent one
lifetime

believing I got born evil, broken, when all I wanted

was mama to rip religion's illegal mattress tag off my life.

Do not question if or why you hate me, only who

taught you how. Would you not also write epistles,

if Consciousness' stream demanded eternal torment

of your loved ones? Why can't my god be proud of what I do?

MOURNING DOVE

Ah, the old atonement—!

That modern banshee scuttles

from the forest floor, startling

the feathery bulk of desiccated leaves

as cicadas preach summer's resurrection.

She mutters her cool, cool, to the damp deciduous
morning,

nostalgia a word she implicitly understands,

her voice echoing the wet grave

of the creek. Why she traded invisibility granted by

underbrush

      —a mystery the hyacinth with its closed
bells finds impossible to solve—

so that a stranger on a screened-in porch may hear
her and dream

of running,

home, barefoot in crabgrass and violets.

mother never watching from the screened-in porch,

but upstairs.

BENEDICTION & CREDITS

Special thanks to my family, both blood and found, who help keep my head above water: Carmen, Edward, Kelsey, Luke, Mina, Oliver, Phillip, Staci, & Tyler;

to Aaron Q., my publisher; and Michael L., and Nate T., my first readers & editors, for believing in all of us, and the arts;

and to our cats, Kiko & Marcel, eternally locked in mortal, divine combat. They (pot, kettle; yin, yang) deserve each other.

"Catalog of Things Lost" and "Fourth of July" first appeared in Walnut Street Branch, issue 1, vol 1. 19 Feb 2024.

"College Poetry Club, En Memoriam" dedicated to M.F. and V.Y., late- former staff members and contributors for The Thorn, Covenant College's undergraduate art magazine.

Rachel E. Krumenacker holds a B.F.A. in English Literature from Covenant College, Lookout Mtn., GA., where her senior class voted her "Most Likely to Publish a Book." Her previous work can be found in The Thorn, The Appalachian Review, and Walnut Street Branch. She has lived in valleys nearby the Appalachian Mountains all her life, and can be found on Instagram and

Threads social media apps under @rkrumcakes.